fast fun & easy

SCRAPBOOK

quilts

Create a Keepsake for Every Memory

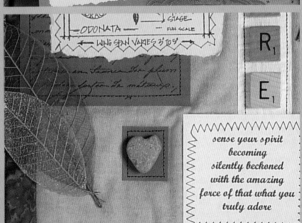

*sense your spirit
becoming
silently beckoned
with the amazing
force of that what you
truly adore*

Sue Astroth

C&T PUBLISHING

Text © 2004 Susan Astroth

Artwork © 2004 C&T Publishing

Publisher: Amy Marson

Editorial Director: Gailen Runge

Editor: Cyndy Lyle Rymer

Copyeditor/Proofreader: Stacy Chamness/Susan Nelsen

Cover Designer: Kristen Yenche

Production Artist: Kirstie L. McCormick

Illustrator: Matt Allen

Production Assistant: Jeff Carrillo

Photography: Sharon Risedorph, Diane Pedersen, and Kirstie L. McCormick unless otherwise noted

Published by C&T Publishing, Inc., P.O. Box 1456, Lafayette, California, 94549

Front cover: Detail of Birthday Girl, Road Trip by Susan Astroth

Back cover: Soccer Quilt, A New Use for Placemats, and Asian Quilt by Suesan Astroth

Attention Teachers: C&T Publishing, Inc. encourages you to use this book as a text for teaching. Contact us at 800-284-1114 or www.ctpub.com for more information about the C&T Teachers Program.

We take great care to ensure that the information included in this book is accurate and presented in good faith, but no warranty is provided nor results guaranteed. Having no control over the choices of materials or procedures used, neither the author nor C&T Publishing, Inc. shall have any liability to any person or entity with respect to any loss or damage caused directly or indirectly by the information contained in this book. For your convenience, we post an up-to-date listing of corrections on our web page www.ctpub.com. If a correction is not already noted, please contact our customer service department at ctinfor@ctpub.com or at P.O. Box 1456, Lafayette, California, 94549.

Trademarked (™) and Registered Trademark (®) names are used throughout this book. Rather than use the symbols with every occurrence of a trademark and registered trademark name, we are using the names only in the editorial fashion and to the benefit of the owner, with no intention of infringement.

Library of Congress Cataloging-in-Publication Data

Astroth, Sue.
  Fast, fun & easy scrapbook quilts : create a keepsake for every memory / Sue Astroth.
    p. cm.
  ISBN 1-57120-252-8 (Paper trade)
  1. Patchwork. 2. Quilting. 3. Assemblage (Art) I. Title: Fast, fun and easy scrapbook quilts. II. Title: Scrapbook quilts. III. Title.
  TT835.A82 2004
  746.46—dc22

                              2003020957

Printed in China
10 9 8 7 6 5 4 3 2 1

Acknowledgments

Dedicated with love to Julia B., Emily B., Lauren B., Melanie P., and Megan P. Always remember you can be anything you want to be; just follow your heart.

This book would not have been possible without the love and support from my family, friends, and a great team of editors at C&T publishing.

I owe bottom-of-my-heart thank yous to:

Mom and Dad for buying me my first sewing machine and always supporting me in everything I do.

Karl and Deena B., for their love and moral support.

Barbara D., my art partner, for your generous heart and creative spirit.

Phyllis N., for allowing me to take yet another day off from work to write a few more words and sew a few more seams.

Gregory, for your talent as an artist and as a friend.

Cyndy R., my editor, for seeing the potential the quilts held and providing me with the opportunity to show them while cheering me on, all the way!

Suze, Paula, Janine, Angie, Kathy, and all the contributing artists for your friendship, and for creating such beautiful pieces of art.

All the students who have taken the Quilted Assemblage (same as Quilted Scrapbook) classes and taught me so much in the process.

To Olaitan, for friendship and for supporting me through my career changes.

Josie and Scott P., for their love and encouragement.

Corey C., for giving up her room so I could have an art studio.

Erin C., for sharing her photos and keeping her music to a dull roar.

And Jois—still!

Fairy Editor, Cyndy Lyle Rymer

Contents

From Quilts to Rubber Stamps
to Scrapbook Quilts

I started quilting some time ago when the country look hit the West Coast. I loved how quilts felt and wanted lots of them. I just didn't have the kind of money needed to buy hand-quilted treasures. I have quilt-top fragments that my maternal Grandmother made, but I wanted big finished quilts to keep me warm at night. So, I started making quilts. First little ones, then as I learned more, the quilts got larger and more artistic.

I love to try any new creative techniques, read art and craft books, and experience different jobs, but I always come back to quilting. So when I needed a birthday present, a quilt was a natural fallback, only this time, it pushed me forward.

Origins of "Scrapbook Pages for Your Walls"

I needed a present for a friend who is a serious stamp/mixed media artist. I knew I couldn't compete with her in the rubber stamp world, but as a quilt artist I could quickly whip up a nifty mini-quilt. Did I mention her birthday was two days away? I had purchased some very cool stamps with face images at a local art stamp show and was anxious to use them. I knew my friend would like them, but I was making a quilt, not a paper project; but hey, why couldn't I combine the two? One thing led to another, and the following picture is the melding of the two mediums.

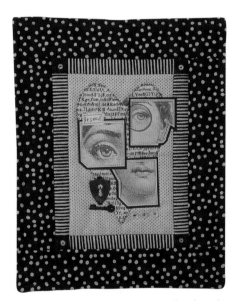

First quilted assemblage or scrapbook quilt

I included images, shapes, and embellishments that were meaningful to both of us. She was surprised, pleased, and, I am proud to say, she hangs it on the door to her studio; that is, when I'm not using it for a class sample.

My friend named her treasure "Quilted Assemblage," and for me a new art form was born. We know what a quilt is, but what in the world is an assemblage? I had heard the term used to describe metal or wood objects, but not fabric, so I looked it up. Besides being a collection of persons or things, it is also considered to be

"an artistic composition made from scraps, junk, and odds and ends (as of paper, cloth, wood, stone, or metal), or the art of making assemblages."

The definition fit and the name stuck. My friend and I talked about what a great product the Quilted Assemblage (QA) was, and how I could teach quilted assemblage art. I had already made a second birthday quilt for a dear friend, and brainstormed about other occasions that could be celebrated with QAs.

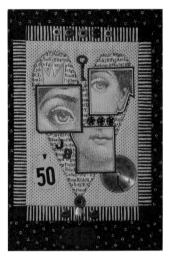

Detail of birthday quilt

Why couldn't we use the small quilt as a way to keep and share memories: a scrapbook page for the wall? After a trip to the fabric store and a raid of my stash, the *Seamstress* quilt (page 30), was born. I gathered my sewing-related stamps, a collection of sewing embellishments, and within a few short hours, I was finished with my new quilted scrapbook page.

Now every time I visit a fabric store I come home with a new combination for a quilt. The sky is the limit. Your budget may be your only limitation.

I hope you find this information useful. Through my work at stamp shows, I've met some wonderful artists. I am very fortunate to be able to share a great collection of their quilted assemblage artwork. I hope these inspire you to make something.

Fabric, Glorious Fabric!

I love buying new fabric. It is so exciting to enter a fabric store and be surrounded by yardage in all directions in every color of the rainbow just waiting for my inspired creations. The fabric designers make it easy to make harmonious fabric selections.

They create a variety of prints, solids, tone-on-tones, and geometric designs all from the same dye lot with the intent to make our lives easier. It helps to know that the colors will match, and the patterns will blend together.

Shopping in Your Jammies

While I love to visit fabric shops and have been known to pick up the yellow pages the minute I hit a new city, I also buy yardage online. At first I was worried about matching designs and colors while Internet shopping. To be honest, I've only been disappointed three times in the five years I have been buying fabric online. Even these less-than-perfect matches can be used on the back of a quilt or traded with friends.

Buying online doesn't mean you stop shopping at your local fabric shops. How else will you get to know the various fabric manufacturer's typical weight, feel, and color tones in their yardage? Besides, hitting the send button doesn't compare to the fabulous sensory overload of walking into your local fabric store.

Did you know you can also find fabric treasures on eBay? The path I follow is to go to crafting and art supply, then fabric. From there I use the search box to better define the item I am looking for. I might type one of the following descriptive words: flowers, feed sack, dress form, hearts, batiks, flannel, and so on. Be as specific as possible; this helps to narrow your choices and prevents too many distractions. Though I must admit, distractions can be a great way to find things you didn't know you needed. Some of my best and favorite finds came from just such a random search. "Vintage" is another good word to use when you are looking for fabrics. Keep in mind that vintage can mean anything from 1930 to 1975. While I have a hard time admitting the 70s are vintage years, it does allow me to see a number of fun treasures I just might need to add to my collection.

Buyer beware! As with most things, if it looks too good to be true, it probably is. If, in the item description, you don't see information you need to know before placing a bid, be sure to ask the seller the question first. Some of the questions I like to ask are: Has the fabric been prewashed?

Do you combine shipping costs on multiple orders? Does the fabric come from a pet-free home. Most importantly, if you are a non-smoker, you should ask if the fabric is coming from a smoke-free home. It's frustrating to receive the perfect fabric in the mail, then finding you need to air it out before you use it because it smells of smoke.

Yes, Garage Sales and Thrift Stores

Another place I find fun fabrics is at garage sales. You may be able to negotiate the price a bit, but most of the above rules apply: Ask first, don't make an insulting offer, and, if it looks too good to be true, it is.

Thrift stores can also provide you with a wealth of fabric at reasonable prices. A little tip: Don't forget to look beyond the craft section of the store. Check out the clothing section. You can find lots of good quality fabric in ready-made garments. Look for interesting prints, natural fabrics, batiks, chiffon, organza, and designer cottons.

For the best value watch for half-price or "one-price bag day." On these special days you fill a bag, usually a large grocery size, and only pay one price on all the clothing items you are able to fit in the bag.

fast! Look for linen shirts. They are great to paint and decorate when you need a designer-look outfit but don't have the budget for designer clothes.

Shirts from local thrift shops

For years quilters have been cutting up clothing to make quilts for practical and sentimental reasons. Many of us know grandmas who saved all the girls' baby dresses to make wedding quilts. Historically, women used whatever fabric they had on hand for their quilts as a matter of thrift. Why not use the same concept for your quilted scrapbook? Check out your stash, closet, and attic to see what you can find. The *Green Girls* quilt was an example of this. It was made from a vintage Girl Scout dress and blouse. Each was well worn and had served the owner well, so I didn't feel too bad about cutting into them to make pieces for the quilt.

The *Green Girls* quilt

The brown fabric that looks just like "brownie" brown is actually a cotton napkin I found at a local thrift shop. This quilt is a tribute to my participation in scouting. One of the great things about quilted scrapbooks is that you can add, change, or update the items on them. I hope my mom and nieces will lend some pictures to add to the *Green Girls* quilt so it can be a family affair.

Types of Fabric

Now that you know where to find fabric, let's talk a bit about what type of fabric to purchase. My preference is good quality 100% cotton fabric because it has a nice feel and is easy to work with. A second choice would be a 100% natural fabric such as linen or silk. The texture and colors usually grab me and find a way into my stash. I have been known to use a poly-blend, but only when the print is so fantastic or the color matches perfectly, that I could not find a cotton to compare.

You are in your sewing room late at night desperately trying to make a project work, but little snags keep cropping up. But, because you are in a hurry (or too stubborn to stop), you keep at it, only to find the next morning you still don't like the finished result? Does this sound familiar? This is what happened while I was making a project for an upcoming scrapbook quilt class. In an effort to break out of my box and provide variety for my students, I used more dramatic fabrics with various prints and stripes. I completed the top, but didn't get the desired dramatic effect. I went to bed, hoping the quilt top would look better by morning light. A new day dawned, and I still didn't like it. In an effort to find the graceful save, I decided to use the top as an example of how **not** to use patterns and stripes in a scrapbook quilt. Wouldn't you know, after showing my students the top and explaining my sad story, they all looked at me and said, "What's wrong with it?"

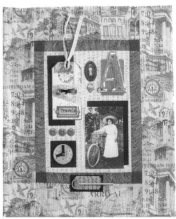

Some of my traditional quilts

Go figure. I share this so you can gain some perspective with my suggestions for combining various fabrics to make a scrapbook quilt. Beauty is definitely in the eye of the beholder.

Fabric Balance

When I first started quilting, I learned that for a quilt to be interesting there should be variety in the size, color, and patterns of the various fabrics. I stuck to very traditional, or "safe," combinations: pink and white, blue and muslin, red and green. I relied on what I liked, and, fortunately, the combinations usually worked.

Some of my traditional quilts

How to Think About Color

I can get all hung up trying to make sure the fabric colors I choose for my next quilt match—exactly. By doing so, I usually lose the feeling of the original quilt I had floating around in my mind, as well as the initiative to see the project through to completion. The beauty of quilted scrapbook quilts is that they are small, easy to piece, and don't require a lot of fabrics. This can make the fabric selection a bit easier. But, being a creative sort, I like options. This usually means a trip to the fabric store, which is fun, but I almost always end up with extra fabric. The color wheel can be a great tool to help in the fabric selection

process; it's inexpensive and something you can do without leaving home.

If I view the color wheel as all the colors of the rainbow, it doesn't seem as intimidating. I don't use a color wheel, but I do know it can be a useful tool to help you confidently choose a color combination for a quilt top or for any art project. Do you always gravitate toward one color section in a fabric store? Another use for the color wheel is to help you break out of your single-color safezone. Here are a few basics to help you off to a good start.

Start with the primary or true colors: your basic red, blue, and yellow. Next, add secondary colors such as orange, green, and purple. It's easy so far, but what about all the colors in between? We know there are more colors; just look at the fabric shelves. The blending of the colors next to each other as they lay on the color wheel creates the colors in between. These are called analogous colors; they will always work well together.

Fabrics that demonstrate the wheel and analogous colors

Here are some other definitions to consider as you select your color scheme of your quilt.
Tint: how much white is in a color
Tone: how much gray in a color
Shade: how much black is in a color

These definitions are important to know while you are selecting individual fabrics so the finished quilt top will match or compliment your overall theme or mood. A darker or muted tone or shade will tend to make the quilt seem more serious while a lighter tint will generate a softer, more delicate look.

Now that you have some basic definitions, let's consider the little quilts we are making in this book. I tend to select a multicolored print for the outer border. By doing so, I usually have a number of colors to choose from, as defined by the multicolored print, for my accent border, squares, and center piece. What happens when you select a border that doesn't have defined additional colors? Take a look at the color wheel: If you start with one color, such as purple for your outer border, you have several options for the other pieces of the quilt. In a monochromatic quilt, each piece of the quilt will vary in value—the lightness or darkness—of purple in this case, from lavender to very deep eggplant.

Another option is choosing the color directly across from purple (or any other color) on the color wheel, which would be yellow. This is called a complementary color. You could use purple for the outer border, yellow for the accent strip, and the squares and center could be a lighter value or tint of yellow or purple.

One last option would be to consider a triadic color combination. Start with any color on the wheel and then take two more colors equal distance away from each other on the wheel.

In the purple example, the two other colors to consider are orange and green.

Here is the most important thing I have to share with you about color: Use fabric and color combinations that make you happy! A color wheel is simply a tool, one of many you can use to make a quilt. It does not define whether or not your quilt is a beautiful or self-fulfilling piece of art. That is up to you; it's in your soul.

Choosing Fabrics for the Base

Scrapbook quilts are made up of three pieces, four if you use a different fabric for the back. The three main pieces are: the center, or base for all the embellishments, the accent strips and corners, and the wide outer border.

The Center

For the center I tend to use a neutral, not-too-busy print or a tone-on-tone fabric. The base is not the star attraction; the embellishments, photos, stamped images, and other treasures convey the overall idea. They will cover the majority of this fabric, so you may not want to use a fancy or more expensive piece of cloth because it won't receive much attention.

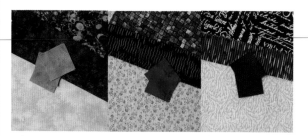

Sample fabric combinations

Accent Strips and Borders

My favorite fabric for the accent strip is a stripe. Stripes add movement to the quilt, and can lend a bit of an "artsy" look. I didn't want to miter corners on the first quilt, so I used complementary squares in each corner. I liked the look and stuck with it for the scrapbook quilts that followed. Sometimes the stripes compete with the final border; if so, try a tone-on-tone and use a third fabric for the accent corner pieces. You can strip-piece the narrow border around the center, but after I started using the accent squares I decided I really liked them. The finished squares provide nice frames for accent buttons, beads, bows, or charms.

Once I make my fabric selection for a scrapbook quilt, I set it in a basket or box so I have a place to gather my embellishments, stamps, or other items until I'm ready to begin the project.

Fabric and embellishments ready to be used in trays

easy! Acrylic picture frames make great affordable cubbies for collecting treasures for a quilt.

Prewashing?

I don't prewash my fabrics. I'm usually too anxious to get started on a project. I figure that since these quilts won't be washed, I don't have to worry about shrinkage. There are always exceptions. I wash fabrics before using them in a quilt if the fabric color is really dye intensive, and if the dye is actually rubbing off on my fingers or the embellishments. I also suggest prewashing fabrics for a bed-size quilt or wallhanging that will be washed regularly.

I treat any clothing I am planning to use in a quilt to a bath first. I wash the garment according to the manufacturer's directions, then iron and hang until I am ready to cut into it. A vintage piece of fabric should be gently bathed on the delicate cycle or by hand. By washing the fabrics first, you ensure that they are ready to use whenever your creative mood strikes (even if it happens to be midnight).

fast! Use a lingerie bag when you use the washing machine for smaller or older pieces of fabric. This minimizes edge fraying and protects your fabric. Another way to prevent edge fraying is to use a zigzag or over-lock stitch around the cut edges of your fabric.

Fabric Selections

I usually select the fabric for the final border first because it's the largest section of the quilt. Try to choose a fabric that will compliment the statement you are making in the quilt. Soft and subtle, distinctive, juvenile, old-fashioned, or retro, the border fabric will really tie it all together.

For the back of the quilt I try to use the same fabric I used in the outer border or at least one in the same color family. This gives the edge of the quilt a finished look.

Scrapbook quilts are made using scrap and treasure collections in my studio. It follows that the batting I use is scraps left over from larger bed and wall quilts. My favorite batting is a blend of 80% cotton and 20% polyester. It is easy to use and adds the traditional look and feel of the vintage quilts I craved when I first began quilting. There are several other low-loft battings available on the market that will give a similar end result.

fun! In a pinch you can also use a good quality, neutral color, double-faced flannel as batting. It has a nice weight and is easy to use. I recommend washing this first.

Embellishing with
Rubber Stamps
and Papers

It's time to admit the ugly truth; I can't draw. I still suffer flashbacks of trying to draw the perfect hand for a science lab paper in seventh grade. I tried and tried for hours to get the right shape and scale of my hand down on the paper. The end result wasn't too bad if you overlooked the out-of-proportion thumb and erasure grooves.

Rubber Stamps: The Challenged Artist's Saving Grace

Fortunately, I discovered rubber stamps. Now I can add artistically executed images at any time to my own artwork, without all the erasure marks.

A basic rubber stamp is made up of three major components: the handle (typically wood), the cushion, and the rubber image or die.

Unmounted Rubber Stamps

Most rubber stamp and craft stores sell rubber stamps already mounted onto wood. These are readily available and very easy to use. If you feel a bit more adventurous, you can purchase unmounted stamps. Unmounteds are a great way to save money, which means you may buy more stamps. If this becomes your method of choice for collecting rubber stamps, you will need a system to temporarily mount the dies. The fastest way, and my favorite method, is to use double-stick tape and an acrylic block. The acrylic block allows you to see through it to the base fabric or paper, which helps to position the image exactly where you want it on the first try. There are many good systems for mounting your stamps. Check the next rubber stamp convention or your favorite online source for more information on the various systems.

A quick way to use unmounted stamps.
Stamps by Oxford Impressions

If you can draw, and have a steady hand, carving your own stamps may be an option. Hand-carved stamps have a rough, artistic, and personal charm to them all their own. Each image is different based on the artist's style and comfort with the carving knife. As with anything, practice makes perfect. So start with simple images and build your confidence.

Carving supplies and stamps.
Stamps by Elaine Beattie

Remember potato carving and stamping in grade school? The same idea applies, only now you have a much wider variety of materials from which to choose: cork, sponges, a good old-fashioned pink eraser, or an artist's carving block made especially for this purpose. Carving your own stamps is an inexpensive way to add to your collection of images. It's also a great way to create that image you can't find ready-made, or if you don't have time to get to a store before your deadline. If you don't want to do your own carving, several stamp companies are manufacturing stamps that are made from original hand-carved images.

One of the best ways (my favorite) to extend your stamp collection is to share with friends. I am fortunate to have a great friend and art partner who lives just under a mile away who is willing to share stamps with me. We take turns buying stamps and other art paraphernalia, and like similar things even though our art is very different. Stamp sharing is a great way to increase our buying power and, more importantly, our creativity. One way to find a friend to share with is to check with your quilt, art, and stamp shops for guilds or clubs in your area. These organizations are great places to meet other artists willing to share or trade supplies, ideas, and inspiration.

easy! The computer can also be a way to connect with other individuals who share a love for stamping or sewing that you do. Do an Internet search for the craft of your choice and you will find a number of sites dedicated to "how-tos," online classes, and e-mail groups.

For most quilted scrapbooks you won't need a large number of stamps. Depending on the theme for an individual quilt, I may use three to four stamped images. If the finished product is more scrapbook/memory related, I use even less. You don't want any one element, fabric or stamp, to overwhelm your finished product.

Inks for Stamping

You can rubber stamp on just about any surface provided you use the right ink. I use several types.

A sampling of inks and paints

Dye-based ink: Dries quickly on absorbent paper, good color selection, sheer, water-based, can be used for stippling or dusting color onto stamped image; clean-up with soap and water.

Pigment-based ink: Must be heat-set on absorbent paper or used with embossing powders, good color selection, opaque, good for creating interesting backgrounds, great for embossing images. Clean-up is easy with soap and water. Use a toothbrush to clean any difficult-to-remove ink.

Permanent inks: Solvent-based, limited color selection, good for stamping on non-porous surfaces; solvent ink cleaner required.

fast! Fabric paints: Acrylic, metallic, all fabric paints can be used with more graphically designed stamps for good results. Use a foam brush and lightly apply paint to the image with a tapping motion.

WORD OF WARNING: Paint can ruin the rubber if it dries on the stamp. Make sure you have a dish with a wet paper towel ready to set your stamp in after you have stamped your design. This will keep the paint wet until you are ready to clean with soap and water.

For most of the images in the book, I used a dye-based ink, typically black, with the exception of a few smaller images I did in color to add a little pizzazz. Occasionally I will stamp the image, then add color to it, by either stippling or "dusting" color onto the image.

Stippling is done by tapping and swirling your brush into a dye-based inkpad, then pouncing the brush onto the paper.

Stippling

The owners of Stampland taught me how to "dust" based on a technique by Judikins (see Sources). For this process you use small, shaving-like brushes pictured below in a sweeping motion over the inkpad to pick up the ink on the outer edges of the bristles. By using the same soft sweeping motion over the paper, you add color to the image. To block areas you don't want to color, use masking paper tape created especially for this purpose or a paper with a low-tack glue that removes easily. This paper tape is readily available in craft, hobby, and art stores.

Dusting

Masking
Stamp by Rubber Cottage

Stamping

To stamp a clean, clear impression follow these steps: Thoroughly ink the stamp for even coverage. Turn over and place the stamp on the paper.

fun! If you are using a stamp that is larger than your stamp pad, simply turn the stamp over and tap the inkpad all over the image.

Move your hand and fingers over the entire image to ensure a good impression. Be careful not to rock the stamp or your image may become blurred. Lift the stamp carefully so the ink is not smeared. Heat set if you are using pigment ink.

Inking a large stamp
Stamp by Post Modern Designs

easy! If you don't get clean stamped images, try placing a mousepad under the paper!

Bird of Beauty, Linda Eustace

You can add interest to a stamped image by embossing it. Using pigment-based ink, ink your selected stamp. Stamp the image onto paper; for best results use non-textured paper. Pour embossing powder over the image, just enough to cover the image. Tap the back of the stamped image to remove powder (save the powder to use later). Then, with a heat tool made specifically for such a purpose, heat the image until the powder melts.

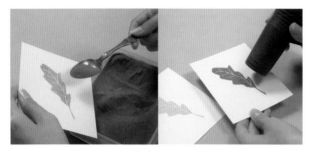

Embossing

Paper Collecting

Collecting paper is like collecting fabric; after all, it is the "fabric" you use for stamping projects. Cards, scrapbook pages, and quilts can all become works of art through the combination of art stamps and beautiful papers. You can find these papers at a variety of stores: art, gift, rubber stamp, craft, scrapbook, and online to name a few. Paper, like fabric, is made with a variety of textures, patterns, and glorious colors to suit your mood or intended project. There are papers with dried flowers imbedded in them, papers with stitching, and even paper that looks like the surface of the moon.

Paper samples

However, with all this paper to choose from, I keep the selection fairly simple for the projects. For my stamped images I use a smooth-surfaced card stock about 60-pound weight in a neutral white or cream. It's fun to create layers of paper by stitching them together. You may want to experiment with vellum, a lightweight translucent paper, by layering it over your photos or stamped images for a dreamy, diffused look.

Sewing on Paper

To sew paper using a machine, I prefer a sharp size 12 needle. Paper can dull needles, so change yours often for smooth stitching. I keep the machine set at 10 stitches to the inch. Too small a stitch may cause your paper to tear. For decorative stitches, such as a zigzag stitch, I may both lengthen and widen the stitch. Play around on your machine with various pieces of scrap paper until you get the result you like best.

fast! Within the last couple years, some of the sewing machine manufacturers are marketing smaller, lightweight (plastic housing) and inexpensive machines to the paper crafters of the world. They are great for taking your project on the road!

Escape from Reality, Phyllis Nelson

Paper Layering

To highlight and accent the stamped image, I may add a layer or two of textured paper. It also adds sparks of different colors to create a "wow" effect in a quilt.

> **fun!** Decorative-edged scissors are another way to add interest to the stamped images or photos on your quilt. Paper punches are also fun to use; try corner rounders for a different look on your photos, or hearts and crown shapes for little accents.

Eyelets

Another fun embellishment that adds a wonderful detail in tiny places are eyelets. Use these little circles of metal to attach papers or photos together and create a finished look on the holes punched in metal or paper tags. They come in a variety of sizes; the most popular size is ⅛" or 3⁄16", and they are available in the entire rainbow of colors. My favorites are the metal colors: brass, pewter, and silver. To add an eyelet you need:

Eyelet and paper
Hole punch
Eyelet setter, universal size
Hammer
Hard surface

Simply punch a hole where you want your eyelet. Place the eyelet in the hole with the unfinished edge of the eyelet to the back of the paper. Lay this on a hard surface with the unfinished edge facing you. Place your eyelet setter in the unfinished edge of the eyelet and hit the end of the setter firmly with a hammer once or twice. The setter gently turns the unfinished edge of the eyelet outward to finish off the embellishment.

Stamp in the Hand

Metallic Papers

Metallic papers are another fun accent. They are available in a variety of thicknesses and shades. Typically these papers are a bit more expensive than most cardstock, but a little goes a long way.

Untitled, Lari Drendell

> **easy!** Using a contrasting color under a keyhole adds an element of surprise and excitement to a simple embellishment.

My Babes, Terrece Siddoway

treasure Hunting

When people ask what I collect, it's hard to come up with a short list. I am easily distracted by fun and interesting objects I didn't know existed or that I needed! In spite of that, I have some basic favorites that friends and I look for whenever we go out treasure hunting. These include vintage sewing notions and buttons, old artist brushes or pens, photography paraphernalia, postcards in a wide variety of topics, and old photographs. Then there is the garden stuff: tools, flower frogs, metal objects, assorted wooden boxes, and, yes, even bowling balls.

2

My family has many names for my treasures; most often they call it junk. They just don't understand! The polite way to describe my obsession is to call me an eclectic collector. Collecting is more than just shopping or stockpiling, as some have referred to my ability for gathering goodies: It's fun!

Friends aren't sure why I still need more seam binding, but I do!

The joy I get from collecting comes in several forms. First, there is the thrill of the find. Uncovering a treasure that fits into an existing collection, or is being offered at a great price, or which I know will make a friend smile, is a wonderful treat. Then there are those glorious moments when you bring home and unwrap the treasure; it's like seeing it for the first time all over again. Next, you (hopefully) find a special spot for it in your home or on an art project. Finally, you are creating great stories to share about how you found it or how little you paid for it, over and over again!

Where to Find Treasures

One of the questions I am asked most often in quilted scrapbook classes is where I find the treasures to add to quilts. The short answer is: Everywhere! Thrift stores, the neighbor's junk drawer, discount stores, sale racks, antique and collectible shops, flea markets, swap meets, and,

of course, Internet auction sites. Whatever your shopping preference, get to know the volunteers or vendors. Shopping can be more fun, and, if you tell them what you are interested in, you have more eyes looking for what you like. Let's face it; collecting treasures is a popular pastime. People you wouldn't expect to treasure hunt do at some time or another. So with all of us out there hunting the good stuff goes quickly! My advice is shop early and often.

fast! You know the fun of finding money on the ground. Don't forget to look around for treasures you may be able to add to a quilt. A piece of wire, a rock in the shape of a heart, or a chain all could work nicely into a scrapbook quilt.

Following is a list of things to look through when you are on a treasure hunt.
Books
Postcards
Magazines, especially vintage
Clothing
Jewelry (whole and parts)
Old office supplies
Paper
Letter tiles from old games
Metal tags
Clothing
Buttons and hardware items

found

easy! Even if you aren't into thrift store clothes, check out the clothing section for buttons and trims. You'll be surprised with what you can find.

Buttons, fabric, trims, paper, and embellishments

Great finds can come from surprising places. These pieces of flatware came from a bit of dumpster diving on our neighborhood's big trash day. The spoons are sterling silver. On other searches we've found old suitcases, bowling balls, and some great old pictures.

Flatware

As a resident of the East Bay area, near San Francisco, I have gained a new respect for recycling. In fact, there are two locations that specialize in recycling and reusing a huge assortment of unlikely items: manufacturing castoffs, egg cartons, fabric samples, manufacturer's over runs, toys, and tools. It's a garage-sale-meets-surplus-store kind of place. The merchandise comes from local business donations as well as estate, garage, or spring-cleaning leftovers from the general public. I never know what I will find, but I always find something I must bring home. Recently we found old percolator parts. These would make great eyes for a scarecrow or frames on a quilt. It all depends on how you look at things.

Check your local yellow pages to see if there are any locations like this in your area. I check the following headings when looking for fun "junk" stores: Salvage, Recycling, Thrift, Reuse, Junk and sometimes even university art departments will sponsor such a store.

Talk with your friends. When they say they are going to do some "spring cleaning," ask to help. Not only do you get the chance for first dibs on some cool stuff, your friend owes you some housecleaning time.

One friend spent a lot of time dealing with an estate, moving heirlooms and treasures to the surviving family members. They eventually reached clean-up, clear-out, and get-rid-of-it mode. Our friend graciously offered what was left over. At first we felt intrusive, but as things got moved to the trash heap, we quickly got over our apprehension. Three carloads later we were finally on our way home. We were thrilled with our treasures, and the family was grateful for the help. They especially enjoyed knowing that someone would enjoy and put to use some of grandpa's collections.

Spread the word that you are a collector; chances are your friends already are aware because you know where all the flea markets, thrift, and junk stores are within a 50-mile radius.

Hardware stores are another place to find interesting décor for your quilts. Screening, hinges, cabinet fixtures, miniature tools, and copper tubing or pipe fittings all make great possibilities for embellishments.

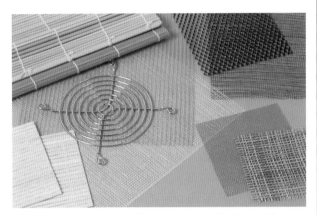

Screening works well as an accent or background.

Don't forget to check your local craft, bead, hobby, scrapbook, or art stamp stores for scrapbook quilt treasures. With the popularity of mixed-media collage work of all kinds, these stores are starting to carry various "found treasures" for your artwork.

The most important thing when looking for treasures is to be open to the potential use of any treasures. When you look at an item, think about what else it could represent. Could you layer two items together? Could it be a frame? Would painting help it? What about the parts of the item? If nothing comes to mind ask a friend. Maybe they will see something entirely different, or maybe they will tell you to put it back and keep shopping. It's all part of the fun of treasure shopping.

What to Do with Photos

When I see old/vintage pictures for sale, I often wonder how families can part with loved one's images of their heritage, but it happens all the time. Families don't write things down. We all keep thinking there is still time to do so, but as they say, "Life is what happens when we are busy making plans." When remaining family members can't recall if the person in the picture is grandpa or the guy down the street, the photo is often discarded. I am a sucker for combing through boxes of old photos for sale. Friends can make it through an entire flea market before I make it to the bottom of a box of photos. Check your stash of family photos for great images to include on a quilt. Interview family members for the who, what, when, where, and how stories behind the images, and record them. I am fortunate to have quite a few family images that I treasure dearly. That doesn't stop me from rescuing other old photos I find while treasure hunting. Some of the images are priceless. Here are some of my favorites.

These can be great to add to your art. Create your own story.

Photocopying Tricks

A great way to extend the life of your photos, family or otherwise, is to photocopy them. Scrapbookers have been doing this for some time. It allows them to alter the size of the picture so it will fit into their decorated page. Copying pictures is easy. Go to your local self-copy store and ask to use the color copy machine. Request brief instructions on the machine so you will know the basics of enlarging, shrinking, and making multiple images on a single page.

Tiled images

The cost is usually minimal: a dollar or less, if you watch for coupons, but plan ahead to make the most of your copy space. Remember: You pay for all the copies you make, even those that don't turn out the way or size you want.

fun! I prefer to use the color copy machine for reproducing my black and white images. I often get a better image than my original. The color copy machine captures all the wonderful colors of age and time that make the vintage picture so dear.

Copyright Alert!
Copying images of your own family is fine. BUT if you copy other images that may or may not be copyrighted, for sale or even for personal use in some situations, you may be stepping on some big toes! Read up on the most recent copyright law at www.nolopress.com. I have found them to be very helpful and informative.

Scrapbooking Treasures

If you don't have the time or the interest to hunt for fabric or other treasures, never fear; scrapbooking and craft companies are here to help. Walk into any craft, hobby, or scrapbooking store and you will find a treasure trove of ready-made goodies just waiting for you.

There are many ready-made embellishments available. Printed paper collages and scrapbook page trinkets are ready to use right from the package. Something is available to suit everyone's taste. You can find a martini glass for your retro look, a paper balloon for a child's birthday quilt, an ivy vine for the graduation remembrance, and everything in between.

Various ready-to-use scrapbooking embellishments.

The Wrap on Wire

Wire is a wonderful way to add dimension and whimsy to your quilt. It is readily available and comes in a variety of colors. You can wrap it around a pencil or similar object for cool spring-like embellishments.

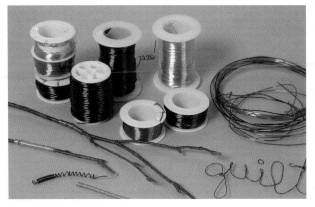

Selection of wire and old wire wrapped around a twig: This is the "good" kind of glitz.

Wrap wire loosely around a picture or other stamped image for an "artsy" look. You can fashion wire into words, either freehand or by using tools available at craft stores. This is a unique way to add words of inspiration or to personalize your artwork.

Beads and Tags

Check out the bead aisle for some wonderful treasures. Beads are a great way to add color or highlight areas on a quilt. String them together to add to a tassel or add a necklace on a picture. You could even sign your scrapbook quilt in beads.

Ascent into Africa, Suze Weinberg and Sue Astroth

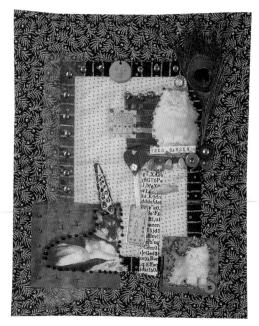

Fred, Hansen, and Anja, Paula Best

Metal tags are another good craft store find, but without the cool patina of old metal tags you might find at flea markets. You can use metal tags as frames, stamp words on them with metal letter or number stamps, ink or stamp images on them with permanent inks, or even use as a charm to hang off the edge of a quilt.

Tags and metal stamps

easy! When you mark tags with metal letters and numbers, make sure to set the tag on a hard, sturdy surface; use a good-quality hammer for a distinct impression.

How to Make the Stunningly Easy Base Quilt

You've collected treasures of all sorts, fabric, embellishments, pictures, and your memories, and even know the best ways to store them. Now that you are ready, let's start working on your own scrapbook (story). Select the fabrics that will best complement the story you wish to tell and let's start sewing. The first step is the quilt base.

Here's what you need to gather before you begin your quilted scrapbook.

Supplies

Sewing machine

Hand sewing needles

Good pair of fabric scissors

See-through ruler with ⅛" marks

Dowel and cording (to hang quilt)

Cotton blend batting, roughly 10" x 15"

Scraps of coordinating fabric (3–5 fat quarters)

Thread

Cutting mat

Rotary cutter

Pins

Cutting

Press all fabrics first before cutting them with a rotary cutter and see-through ruler.

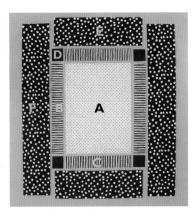

Quilt base

A: 1 rectangle 9½" x 7" from your lightest fabric

B: 2 strips 1¼"-wide x 9½"

C: 2 strips 1¼"-wide x 7"

D: 4 squares 1¼" x 1¼"

E: 4 strips 3" x minimum 16"

Hanging sleeve (on back of quilt) 3½" x 10" contrasting fabric for hanging pocket (on back)

Sewing

1. Sew a B strip to each side of the center rectangle A. Finger-press seams away from the center square.

2. Sew a D to each end of both piece C's.

3. Attach the pieced borders to center piece at top and bottom. Press.

4. Sew the E border to top and bottom of quilt; trim. Sew remaining border E's. Trim and press. Square up.

5. Lay the batting on the table in front of you. Lay the backing piece face up on top of the batting. Lightly press.

6. Lay the pieced top face down on the backing fabric. Pin.

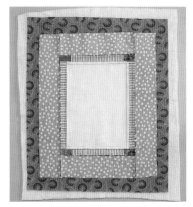

Batting, backing, and quilt top layered together.

7. Using the edge of your top as a guide, sew around the quilt using a ¼" seam. Leave a 2½"–3" opening at the bottom of the quilt for turning right side out. Trim away excess threads and batting (close to seam allowance).

Trim close to the seam allowance.

Clip the corners diagonally. Turn the quilt right side out and lightly press. Pin opening and sew closed by hand with a hidden stitch.

8. To hold the layers together, machine quilt around the quilt ¼" from the edge of quilt. Also quilt in-the-ditch (right along the seam allowance) between the two borders and centerpiece.

Congratulations, your quilt base is complete! But you have only told half your story. To complete your story you need to gather all your treasures, charms, pictures, and stamped images. But, before we start embellishing, let's talk a little about a composition plan.

Quilt Before You Embellish

Quilting scrapbook quilts is simple. All you really need to do is stitch-in-the-ditch between the borders and the center. If you are really ambitious, you can do more quilting, such as free-motion quilting around a design pattern in the outer border. You can elect to make the outer borders wider to feature your beautiful quilting.

Composing Your Memories

People often ask how I pull together all the various photos, colors, and embellishments to create the design on a quilt. There is no easy answer because so much of the design is decided or dictated by the specific embellishments I want use to tell a particular story. As I was searching for a way to write about this, I began looking at the quilts with a critical eye toward the individual elements. How many of the elements on each quilt actually were part of the quilt's story? I was surprised to find out that less than half of the treasures sewn to a quilt are critical or key elements to the story.

fast! Framing an element is one way to insure the element will be "key" on your quilt top.

Key Elements

Usually the key elements are the largest pieces or comprise the largest section on a quilt top, but they are outnumbered by "filler" elements, on average, three to one. Fillers are elements that peripherally enhance the design in some fashion or creatively fill an open space on the quilt. You have to decide what the key elements are as they are specific to the story. Here is a list of some of the filler items I regularly use:

Keys	Washers
Leaves	Optical lenses
Charms	Watch faces
Buttons	Game pieces
Snaps	Metal tags
Stars	Crowns
Rulers	Hearts

note Some filler elements may be considered key elements depending on your theme. Snaps and buttons are such items. They are key on the Seamstress quilt (page 30), but on the 50th birthday quilt (page 5) they add dimension and interest in an unrelated way.

Once I decide what elements I want to use, I play with several layouts until I decide what I like best. While working on the *Seamstress* quilt, a quilting buddy who worked on the school yearbook told me to keep the action moving inward on the quilt. This keeps the focus on the center or whole quilt. Being a bit of a doubting Thomas, I tried the stamp a couple of ways and wouldn't you know, she was right!

On the *Cowgirl* quilt (page 40) I challenged that rule a bit. While I do have the picture of the girl facing out to the left, she is held in place by the bolo tie. This keeps all of the elements together and, to my eye, centered.

I also try to keep to the rule of "Odd numbers are more interesting." I use buttons in rows of three or five. I arrange the entire quilt using either one large key element or three smaller ones. Even the *Inspiration* quilt (page 35) fits this model because there are three key words with one key element. The goal is to balance your quilt.

Once you start collecting your embellishments you will probably end up with more treasures than will actually fit on your quilt. While it will be difficult to eliminate, you have to be selective with what you include on the quilt. Another rule of thumb I follow is "less is more." Too many little things tend to make the quilts look too busy. By selecting only the best key and filler elements you make a more defined statement. If you just have to include a bunch of little things consider grouping them together on a background of cardstock. This creates a more power single image rather than a scattering of little ones.

On the off chance you don't have enough embellishments or are giving the quilt to someone with a "minimalist" style, you may consider adding an appliqué, with a contrasting fabric, to the background before you start adding your treasures. This creates a subtle effect and helps to minimize the area you need to embellish.

Too busy. Less is more.

One of the best suggestions I can give you when working on your quilt is to take breaks. Lay out the design you think you want, then walk away and take a well-deserved break. When you come back to the studio, you will look at the quilt with fresh eyes and if it makes you smile, you are ready to sew everything in place. If you find you aren't smiling, try another layout or switch some of the elements you originally selected. Frequently, the first plan I had in my head isn't what ends up on the quilt. Once the creative process begins to flow, you need to follow where it takes you. You just might surprise yourself.

Easy! Scrapbook magazines are a great place to get ideas for layouts or combinations for your quilt tops.

Trip for my Father, Barbara Delap

Stampland

Here are some layout suggestions for a well-balanced quilt.

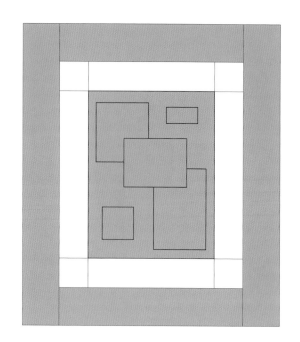

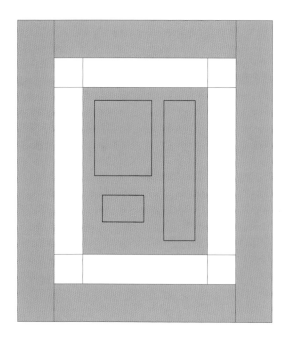

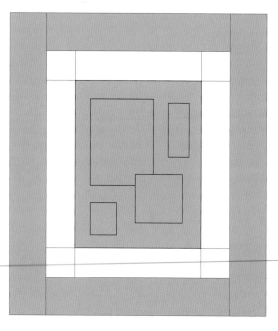

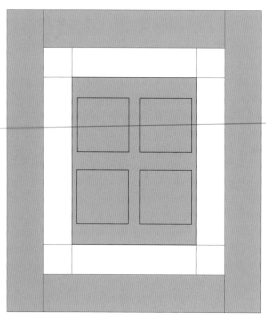

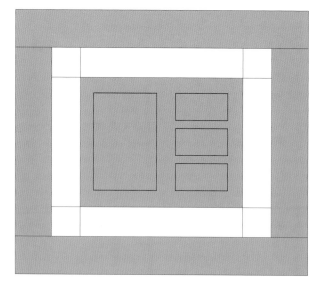

Composing Your Quilt

Now you are ready to compose your quilt using all of the treasures you have gathered.

Select the key elements you plan to use on the quilt and place them on the quilt top. Audition and add various embellishments and fillers until it is pleasing to your eye.

Next, stamp the images you selected onto card-stock or fabric. Trim close to the image, leaving a very small border around it. The border is the area you will use to sew the image onto the quilt.

I like the look of framed images so I layer my stamped images with a complementary colored cardstock. You can also outline the layering with a chisel-tipped metallic gold pen for a bit of glitz. Remember to let the ink dry before you lay the image on your fabric.

Once you have stamped all your images lay them down on the quilt top. Add all your other embell-ishments once more to make sure you wind up with the design you want.

Playing in The Kelp, Janie Anderson

Sewing Plan

Now it's time to create a sewing plan. Assign an order to each item to be sewn onto the quilt. This is important because you are working with items that don't have any "give" to them, such as paper, metal, wood, and so on. The plan makes its easier to work on the sewing machine, and all of the elements will stay in the chosen place.

fast! Add a small amount of adhesive on the edges of the wrong side of the cardstock to keep it in place while sewing it onto the quilt.

Road Trip, Susan Astroth

Seamstress Quilt

I was fortunate to find this fabric that depicts old labels; it really makes this quilt. Once I selected that fabric, the center called out to be a shirtwaist stripe. This quilt would make a perfect gift for a quilting or sewing friend, or a nice companion in your work space.

Materials

- Stamps: small alphabet, mannequin, thimble, fall suits (or equivalent)
- Cardstock: black, cream
- Ink: black, gold metallic
- Plastic scissors (I painted the handles with black acrylic paint to more closely resemble the scissors I first used when I learned to sew.)
- Vintage black rayon seam binding
- Vintage crochet piece
- Old watch face
- Vintage photo pin back
- Old ruler (This one is actually from an old typewriter.)
- Brass eyelets
- Old thread labels
- Assorted vintage buttons and snaps
- Foam dots

Design and Sewing Plan

1. Stamp all images on cardstock, stamping the Fall Suits image twice. Trim and set aside.

2. Trim the black and cream cardstock around the stamped images. Cut out the image of the woman from the second Fall Suits you stamped.

3. Use your sewing machine to add the Fall Suits, then the mannequin image.

4. Sew some black seam binding ribbon tails by hand to the wrong side of the crochet piece. They will show when you sew the crochet piece in place. Hand sew the ruler and crochet piece to the quilt.

5. Arrange the watch face, buttons, snaps, and thread labels under the Fall Suits image. Sew in place.

6. Sew scissors onto the quilt top.

7. Place eyelets on the "stitch in time" tag and sew to quilt by hand.

8. Secure the thimble to black cardstock with a foam dot to add dimension and hand sew onto quilt.

9. Add second image of woman from the Fall Suits image over the original with foam dots for additional dimension.

10. Add a label to the back of the quilt.

Teacher Appreciation

This quilt makes a great present for a teacher. You could add well wishes from all the students, and maybe include their finger- prints for fun. This also works well as a scrapbook to celebrate a child's accomplishments.

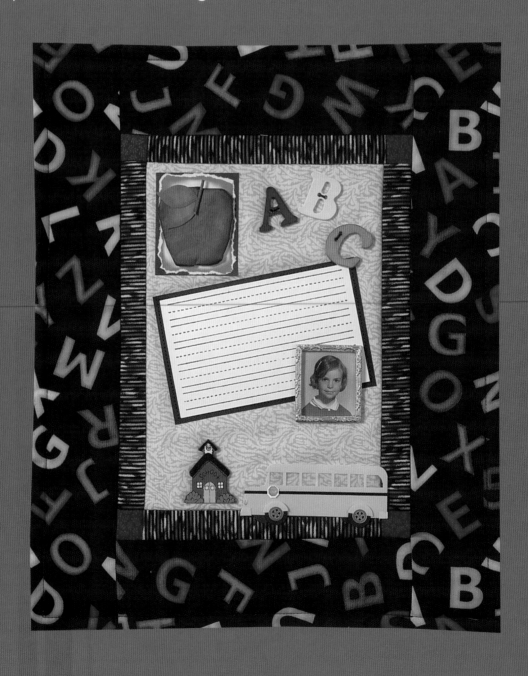

Materials

- ☐ Stamps used: grade-school writing paper
- ☐ Cardstock: white, black
- ☐ Copy of school photo (a teacher's or a student's photo)
- ☐ ABC buttons
- ☐ Ready-made embellishments, such as an apple and/or bus
- ☐ Gold metal frame

- ☐ Ready-made wooden school house
- ☐ For pocket on back:
  School paper
  Apple button
  Vintage yellow seam binding
  Eyelets
  Safety pins
- ☐ Glue dots
- ☐ Adhesive

Design and Sewing Plan

1. Stamp Grade school writing paper on cream cardstock. Trim and layer on black cardstock. Sew by machine to quilt.

2. Sew with machine small strip of black cardstock to quilt where bus will be attached.

3. Attach schoolhouse, apple, frame, and bus with glue dots.

4. Hand sew ABC buttons to quilt.

5. Make paper pocket (see page 45) for back of quilt. Add eyelets to top corners to hang on back with safety pins.

6. Add the yellow seam binding and apple button to a ready-made tag for fun.

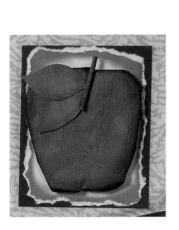

Asian Quilt

I made this quilt for my friends at Stampland in Chicago. I loved the Geisha image and wanted a way to highlight her. I'm pleased with the results. Notice how I fussy-cut the accent corners so the language characters would fit in the square.

Materials

- Stamps used: Geisha, simple pleasures (or other quote stamp)
- Cardstock: cream, black
- Joss paper (available at Asian markets or specialty art stores)
- Chopstick
- Woven mat 3½" x 3½" (pieces of old woven placemats work well)
- Number game tile

- Button
- 3 Asian coins
- Black perle cotton thread (or embroidery thread)
- Gold chisel-tip metallic ink pen
- Red cording for bow
- Small drill

Design and Sewing Plan

1. Stamp images on cream cardstock and trim.

2. Edge the stamped and trimmed cardstock with the gold metallic pen. Let dry.

3. Layer stamped images onto black cardstock and trim, leaving a small frame around the edges.

4. Lay the woven mat on quilt at an angle. Using the photo as a guide, lay the Geisha image on woven mat and sew onto quilt.

5. Fold Joss paper just around center image, and trim away excess. Sew to quilt.

6. Place Simple pleasures image on quilt and sew in place.

7. Drill a hole through the game tile and place on quilt. Position button over drilled holes and hand sew both to quilt.

8. Lay out coins and hand sew to quilt using the perle cotton.

9. Sew loops around the chopstick ¼" from the top and bottom of the stick through to the quilt.

10. Tie bow on chopstick.

Cowgirl

This is a just-for-fun quilt. I had some red and brown scraps left over from another project, and then found the photo of the cowgirl. The bolo tie added just the right touch to the finished quilt.

Materials

- ☐ Stamps used: frame, small alphabet, yee-haw
- ☐ Cardstock: cream, kraft brown, red, black, and gold
- ☐ Ink: black, metallic gold, brown
- ☐ Gold embossing powder
- ☐ Color copy of a vintage photo
- ☐ Leather bolo tie
- ☐ Vintage wooden nickel

- ☐ Vintage horse charm
- ☐ Red satin ribbon
- ☐ Toy sheriff badge
- ☐ Black ¼" silk ribbon
- ☐ Belt charm
- ☐ Vintage bottle cap
- ☐ 3 metal star buttons
- ☐ 3-D glue dots

Design and Sewing Plan

1. Trim color copy of photo with deckle-edge scissors and mount on gold cardstock. Trim.

2. Cut a square 1½" x 1½" and a 1" circle of black cardstock and sew to quilt as an accent for the bottle cap and wooden nickel.

3. Sew a 3" x 4½" rectangle to quilt as a base for the photo.

4. Use small alphabet stamps and black ink to stamp on the kraftbrown cardstock.

5. Stamp the frame on red cardstock in metallic ink; emboss with gold detail powder (see page 16). Cut out.

6. Cut stamped text to fit outer edge of frame and sew to quilt.

7. Attach the picture and wooden nickel to the quilt using large glue dots.

8. Glue bottle cap and badge to quilt using glue dots.

9. Arrange bolo tie around photo and sew in place by hand.

10. Loop ribbon through belt charm and attach to bolo tie using a 3-D glue dot.

11. Sew star buttons in place.

Write Your Own Story

One day when I was supposed
to be working on the text for this
book, I wanted to play with fabric instead. This is the result.

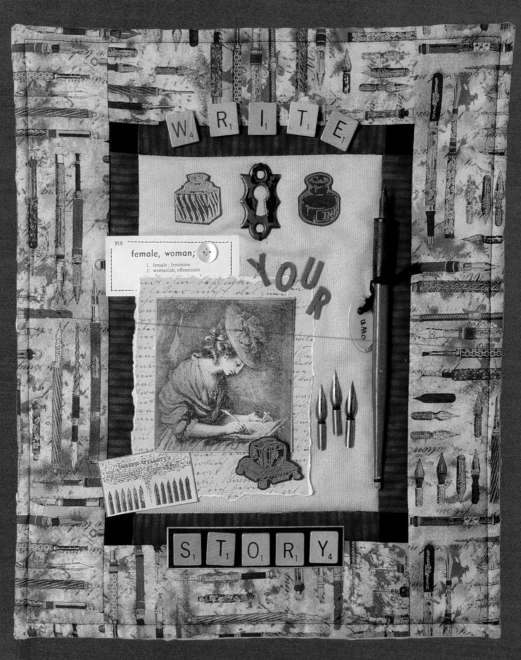

Materials

- ☐ Stamps: woman at writing desk, small alphabet, various inkwells
- ☐ Cardstock: cream, black
- ☐ Ink: black, ochre, mauve, straw, and metallic gold
- ☐ Gold embossing powder
- ☐ Gold chisel-tip metallic ink pen
- ☐ Photocopy of old letter and vintage pen ad
- ☐ Vintage vocabulary card
- ☐ Pearl button
- ☐ Vellum oval tag
- ☐ Vintage pen nibs
- ☐ Vintage calligraphy pen
- ☐ Keyhole
- ☐ Game letters
- ☐ Vintage red plastic letters
- ☐ Black eyelet
- ☐ Glue
- ☐ Foam dots

Design and Sewing Plan

1. Stamp inkwells on black cardstock in metallic ink. Emboss with gold detail powder (see page 16).

2. Stamp lady image, script background, and "own" on vellum tag in black ink.

3. Dust mauve, straw, and ochre colors onto lady image, then trim.

4. Tear the edges of the photocopied letter to fit behind the lady image.

5. Sew vocabulary card onto quilt.

6. Stitch background onto quilt using zigzag stitch.

7. Cut a 1" x 4½" strip of black cardstock. Edge the cardstock with metallic gold pen. Allow the ink to dry, then sew to the bottom of the quilt for the "story" letters.

8. Cut out small squares of black cardstock. Sew to the top of the quilt so you can glue the inkwells and "write" letters to the quilt.

9. Sew keyhole, pen, and pen nibs to quilt by hand.

10. Attach lady image with foam dots.

11. Attach bottom inkwell and pen nib ad with foam dots.

12. Sew "your" letter to quilt by hand.

13. Glue pearl button, letters, and last two inkwells onto quilt.

14. Attach black eyelet to vellum tag (see page 17), string with black ribbon, and hang on pen.

Hawaii Revisited

This quilt was made as a remembrance of a very special trip. The fabric, which was originally earmarked for a shirt, was perfect!

Materials

- Stamps: Hawaiian Islands, tiki, Hawaii montage, graphic square, and "Hawaii"
- Cardstock: green, blue, cream, red
- Ink: brown, black
- Thread: red, brown
- Brown ribbon
- Manila tag envelope
- Hawaiian shirt luggage tag
- Straw (part of an old placemat works when you want to add some texture)
- Silver label frame
- Vintage coconut-shell fish pin
- Shell lei
- Small drill
- Foam dots
- Glue

Design and Sewing Plan

1. Stamp Hawaiian Islands, Aloha, and "Hawaii" in brown ink on cream cardstock.

2. Tear out Hawaiian Islands and Aloha images. Stipple images with brown ink around edges for an aged look.

3. Stamp graphic design in black; stipple with brown ink in center. Trim.

4. Card stock: Cut a 1" x 6" piece of red, a 4" x 5" piece of green, and a 1½" x 3½" piece of blue. Sew these to the quilt using brown thread.

5. Add straw mesh at an angle under the red strip of cardstock.

6. Drill two small holes on the collar and one on the bottom corner of the shirt luggage tag. Sew the tag to the quilt by hand with red thread.

7. Sew the graphic square image to the top of the red cardstock by machine.

8. Lay the label frame over the "Hawaii" image; trim. Sew by hand onto the quilt.

9. Use foam dots to attach the "Aloha" image to blue cardstock.

10. Glue the map of Hawaii to the green cardstock.

11. Arrange the shell lei over the entire design. Pin in place and sew it to the quilt by hand.

Back Pocket

1. Using black ink, stamp the manila envelope with the Hawaii montage stamp.

2. Using brown ink, stamp the tiki image on cream cardstock. Tear out and stipple brown ink lightly over the entire design. Trim.

3. Tear a strip of green cardstock approximately ½" wide and glue it along the top of the stamped image.

4. Cut a 1⅝" x 3" piece of blue card stock. Use a foam dot to attach the tiki stamp onto the blue cardstock. Glue the entire piece onto the envelope.

5. Stamp "Hawaii" sideways directly onto the envelope in black ink.

6. Write the year of your trip directly below "Hawaii."

7. Hand stitch brown ribbon to the quilt back, then tie it to the envelope.

The Green Girls

This is a memory quilt of my happy times in scouting. I found an old uniform that was a bit weary so I decided to use it, along with an old Girl Scout shirt for the center. It created a great frame for some special memories.

Materials

- Cardstock: green
- Color copies of "vintage" Girl Scout photos and ID card
- Troop numbers
- Uniform buttons
- Various patches
- Membership pins
- Vintage green rayon seam binding
- Scout charm
- Thread: brown, green
- Brownie pocket
- Glue

Design and Sewing Plan

1. Trim the photo with deckle-edge scissors and glue onto green cardstock.

2. Trim the ID card and scout photo; glue onto green cardstock.

3. Sew photos and ID card to quilt with green thread.

4. Use brown thread to add troop numbers.

5. Add wings and other patches by hand or machine using green thread.

6. Sew buttons in place with green thread.

7. Add membership pins.

8. Make a bow from seam binding. Attach the bow to the charm. Sew in place by hand with green thread.

I placed the pin from the felt patch on the front so it holds the brownie pocket on the back, and put the dress label on the back.

Think Art!

Working in my studio one night, I started pulling out some favorite stamps while I struggled to come up with a theme for a class sample. I kept saying, "Think art, think art." Hey, Think Art!

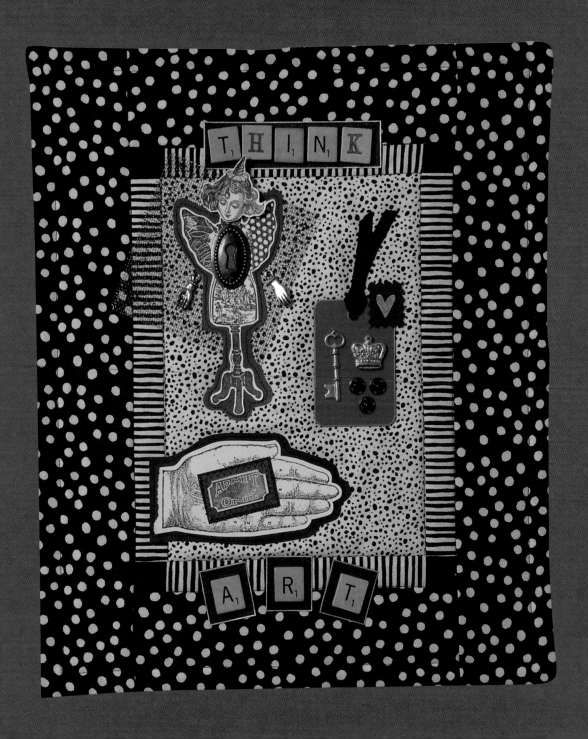

Materials

- Stamps: doll head, Paris mannequin, open hand, Admit One, small heart, alphabet
- Cardstock: textured black, textured red
- Ink: black, mauve, white pigment, red permanent
- Glue dots
- Foam dots
- Game letter tiles
- Keyhole
- Charms: hands, crown, key
- Formica sample tile
- Gold chisel-tip metallic ink pen
- Gold mesh
- Black seam binding
- Snaps
- Glue

Design and Sewing Plan

1. Stamp the hand, mannequin, and doll head in black ink on cream cardstock. Cut out. Note: I tore the hand just for a bit of interest.

2. Glue the mannequin to red cardstock, except for the head. Trim, leaving enough red border so you can stitch it to the quilt. Use a foam dot to attach the doll head to the mannequin. Trim as needed.

3. Glue the hand to black textured cardstock; trim so there is enough of a border to sew it to the quilt.

4. Stamp "Admit One" in mauve ink on cream cardstock. Cut out.

5. Cut a square 1¾" x 1¾" of black cardstock, and a slightly smaller red piece. Zigzag stitch onto the hand.

6. Cut 3 pieces 1¼" x 1⅛" of black cardstock, edge with gold metallic ink. Let dry, then sew to the bottom of the quilt.

7. Cut a 1¾" x 2¾" piece of black cardstock. Sew in place for the Formica tag.

8. Cut a 1" x 4¼" piece of black cardstock. Edge with gold metallic ink and sew to top of quilt.

9. Lay the screening on the quilt at an angle. Sew by machine using a zigzag stitch.

10. Sew mannequin over mesh; go slowly so your stitches are even.

11. Edge the Formica tile with gold metallic ink pen. Let dry.

12. Stamp letters onto the game letter tiles with permanent red ink. Heat set.

13. Stamp a small heart onto black card stock; cut out with decorative-edge scissors.

14. Slipknot seam binding through the Formica tag. Use glue dots to attach the tag to cardstock.

15. Use glue dots to attach the letters to cardstock.

16. Use foam dots to attach the doll head, Admit One, and crown to the quilt.

17. Sew hands onto mannequin.

18. Attach red cardstock to the back of the keyhole. Trim and sew to quilt by hand.

19. Glue snaps and key to tag; let dry.

20. Attach small heart to tag with a glue dot.

Baby Quilt

This is a memory quilt celebrating the birth of a dear friend's daughter, Erin Marie. She's a bit older and 5'10" now, but still her mom's little girl.

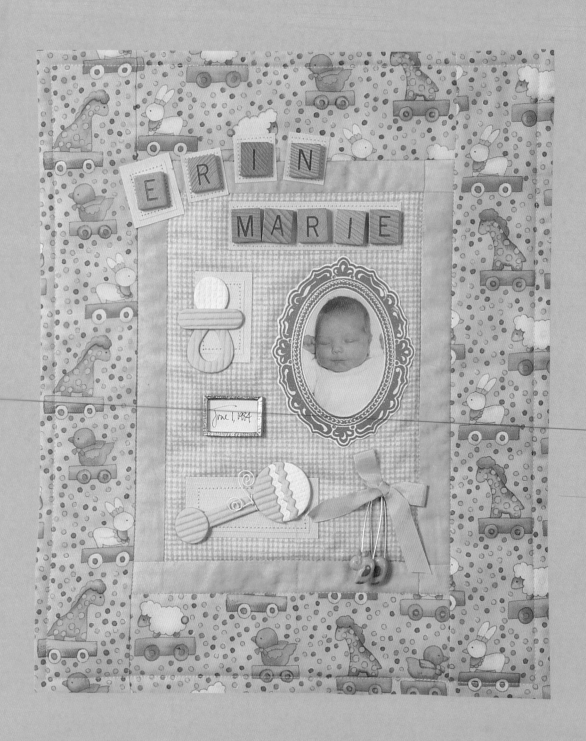

Materials

- ☐ Stamps used: gold frame
- ☐ Ink: gold
- ☐ Cardstock: cream, light yellow textured, light pink textured
- ☐ Color photocopy of a baby picture
- ☐ Gold embossing powder
- ☐ Vintage seam binding
- ☐ Old diaper pins
- ☐ Ready-made embellishments, such as rattle and pacifier
- ☐ Gold frame
- ☐ Old game letter tiles
- ☐ Glue

Design and Sewing Plan

1. Stamp gold frame on cream cardstock and emboss with gold. Cut out around edge both inside and out.

2. Trim photo to match the size of the frame, leaving enough room to sew to the quilt with a seam that will be hidden by the frame. I layered the photo to an unseen piece of cardstock for more stability when sewing the photo to the quilt.

3. Cut out cardstock to highlight the ready-made embellishments, frame piece, a small piece hidden behind the gold frame and letter tiles.

4. Following sample photo, lay out cut cardstock and sew to quilt.

5. Glue letter tiles, ready-made embellishments, and frame to quilt.

6. Tie bow through the ends of the diaper pins and sew to quilt.

7. Cut small piece of cream cardstock and write baby's birthday on it, trim and place in gold frame.

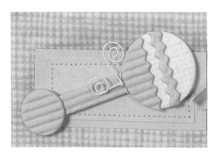

"Cutie Pie"

Nature
Appreciation

I bought this gorgeous batik fabric a couple of years ago at the International Quilt Festival in San José. Everyone was into stamped fabrics and I just had to have some. The dragonflies really appealed to me. At the time I had no idea what they would become. I just love the result!

Materials

- Stamps used: dragonfly, script, letter set

- Cardstock: dark green, textured light green, and cream

- Crown charm

- Your favorite poem or quote

- Green and gold skeleton leaves (sold in packages as a ready-made embellishment; looks like what they are called)

- Heart-shaped rock

- Game letter tiles to spell NATURE

- Twig

- Rectangle metal-rimmed tag

- Metal file frame

- Adhesive

- Thick white glue

Design and Sewing Plan

1. Following the photo, stamp the dragonfly and quote/poem on cream cardstock, and the script on dark green.

2. Trim script and stamped images. Leaving about ¼" around the design, sew onto the quilt.

3. Tear edges of dragonfly image.

fun! For an interesting edge, when tearing paper, remember to pull the excess paper toward you. This leaves a rough, random edge on the piece you want to add to your art.

4. Cut a small square of dark green cardstock to fit behind your heart rock.

5. Cut a 11¼" x 6½" piece of light green textured cardstock.

6. Following the photo, sew script, the small square of green cardstock, the light green cardstock, and the stamped image to the quilt top.

7. Sew dragonfly to script using a zigzag stitch.

8. Sew the twig and metal frame to quilt.

9. Write "botanical" on a scrap of cream cardstock and slip behind the metal frame.

10. Stamp "fig. #3" on metal-rimmed tag and tie around twig.

11. Glue crown, letter tiles, and rock in place. Let dry.

12. Place a thin line of glue on the largest veins of each leaf and place on the quilt. You can also take very, very tiny stitches along the vein to hold the leaves in place.

easy! When fitting a specific word onto cut cardstock with letter tiles, start with the middle letter and work your way out to both ends. This way you are sure to have enough room to fit the entire word where you want it.

Grandma Was a Flag Waver

The Fourth of July is one of my favorite holidays. I just love red, white, and blue. I pieced the top out of some scraps I had around the sewing room. Then I found the picture of the "grandma with a flag." The title/story wrote itself.

Materials

- ☐ Cardstock: textured black, textured blue, textured red
- ☐ Color photocopy of vintage photo of woman with flag, man in uniform
- ☐ Color photocopies of ration book page, coupons, and thrift stamps
- ☐ Medal ribbon (I used an old swimming award ribbon and removed the swim medal.)

- ☐ Two red, white, and blue pins
- ☐ 3 tiny pearl buttons
- ☐ Transportation token
- ☐ Cross charm
- ☐ 3 vintage paper tokens
- ☐ Glue

Design and Sewing Plan

1. Cut out grandma photo with deckle-edge scissors. Glue to black cardstock and trim.

2. Cut out ration book photocopy and adhere to blue cardstock. Cut out, leaving enough room to zigzag stitch to quilt.

3. Cut out the man in uniform and glue to red cardstock. Cut approximately ¼" from the image so he is outlined in red.

4. Sew grandma, the ration book, and man in uniform to quilt.

5. Cut a piece of blue cardstock to fit behind the thrift coupons and sew to quilt.

6. Cut tiny pieces of blue cardstock and sew to quilt where you want to place the 3 paper tokens and single thrift stamps.

7. Hand sew buttons and cross in place.

8. Pin on the medal ribbon and little star pin to quilt.

9. Following the photo, glue all tokens in place.

Ration book pages may be available in collectible shops.

Soccer Quilt

Soccer players of all ages will love this quilt! If you can't find soccer fabric for the outer border, consider stamping a solid fabric with a soccer ball stamp.

Another idea is to place photos of a favorite coach or the entire team on the front or back of the quilt.

Materials

- ☐ Stamps used: small alphabet
- ☐ Cardstock: cream, red, black, and purple
- ☐ Color copy of soccer picture
- ☐ Bamboo skewer
- ☐ 24-gauge purple wire

- ☐ Sheer ¼" black ribbon for bow
- ☐ Vintage metal letters
- ☐ 2 label frames
- ☐ Soccer event participation pins
- ☐ Paint: black acrylic

Design and Sewing Plan

1. Trim soccer picture and layer onto black and team-colored card stock. Sew onto quilt.

2. Cut a 5½" x 1¼" piece of black cardstock and a 5" x 1¼" piece of cardstock in team colors.

3. Sew black cardstock onto quilt, then team color piece.

4. Cut a random pennant triangle out of red cardstock and smaller team color piece to accent.

5. Use the machine to stitch a red triangle to a bamboo skewer with a zigzag stitch.

6. Wrap the base of the bamboo skewer with team-colored wire.

7. Sew skewer to quilt by hand.

8. Stamp words to fit into label frames.

9. Sew label frames to quilt by hand.

10. Add soccer pins to quilt top.

Optional: Using alphabet stamps, stamp team statistics on paper and sew to back of quilt.

The No-Sew Version:
A New Use for Placemats

If you are in a hurry, use a placemat for the base rather than making the quilted base. Look for a simple placemat that will enhance your design. All of the elements can be attached using a glue gun or glue dots, or white glue. For this piece, I chose cotton duck, which is easy to glue things onto and has enough body to hang without curling.

Materials

- ☐ Stamps: Bird nest
- ☐ Cardstock: green, light green, brown kraft tag, cream
- ☐ Ink: green
- ☐ Photo
- ☐ Assorted metal letters
- ☐ Twigs
- ☐ Vintage key and keyhole
- ☐ Cotton duck placemat

- ☐ 24-gauge wire
- ☐ Die-cut trees
- ☐ Large metal charms of leaves and dragonfly
- ☐ Background mesh
- ☐ 6" jute cord or twine
- ☐ Adhesive
- ☐ Glue gun
- ☐ Glue dots

Design and Sewing Plan

1. Fold under the top edge 3" and glue to the back side of the placemat along the sewn edge. This creates a pocket that enables you to hang the quilt on a dowel, ruler, curtain rod, or, as in this case, a tree branch.

2. Center mesh on the front of the placemat.

3. Glue the photo to the gold cardstock with adhesive and trim cardstock to ⅛" around photo.

Note: The bottom edge of the cardstock was torn when I received it. I liked the look and kept it for one of the edges around the photo.

4. Cut a piece of green cardstock 6 ¾" x 4 ½".

5. Glue large metal charms to the cardstock.

6. Tear a piece of cream cardstock roughly 6 x ¾". Glue to the cut piece of green cardstock.

7. Arrange and attach letters to cream cardstock with glue dots.

8. Stamp bird nest on Kraft-brown cardstock. Trim along the image, leaving ⅛" around the edge. Place on a 3" x 3" piece of green cardstock.

9. Tear a 1" x 2 ½" piece of light green cardstock and glue to Kraft-brown tag. Glue the keyhole to the tag.

10. Tear a 1" x 2 ¾" piece of light green cardstock as a backing for the key.

11. For a touch of the unexpected, I added 24-gauge wire around a small area on the twig.

Now you have all your elements put together. Follow the photo and arrange them on your placemat. Glue in place. The mesh has a large open weave, so I didn't glue it by itself. I let the glue from the other elements hold it in place.

Variation: The Studio Quilt

My studio is at the end of a long hall. Seeing this on the door creates a delicious sense of anticipation: Oh, the possibilities of what I can create!

The finished size of this quilt is 14" x 25", a bit longer than the original scrapbook quilt so it looks more balanced on a door.

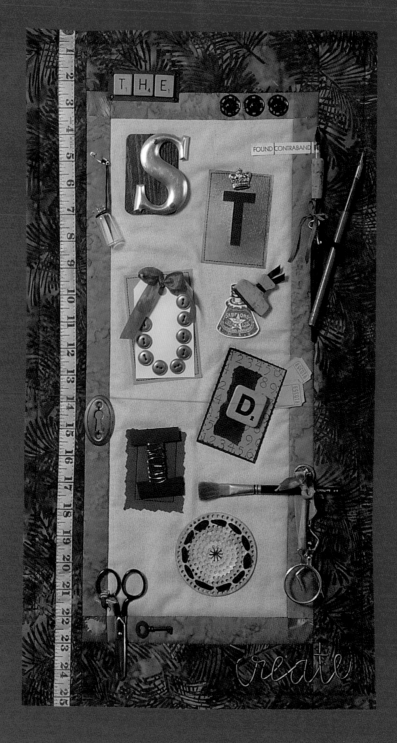

Materials

The pattern piece sizes for this quilt are:

- ☐ Centerpiece: 18½" x 7½"

- ☐ Accent border: 2 pieces 1½" x 7½" and 2 pieces 1½" x 20½"

- ☐ 4 small squares: 1½" x 1½"

- ☐ Outer border: 2 pieces 3½" x 9½" and 2 pieces 3½" x 25½"

- ☐ Back and batting: at least 16" x 27"

The basic sewing plan for this base quilt is the same as the original.

Use your imagination and your stash of found treasures to make your own version of this quilt. For embellishments, I used a variety of treasures that might be inside an artist's studio.

I found the tape measure in an old sewing kit. I stippled it with dye-based ink to tone down the brightness. To protect the surrounding fabric I placed scrap notepaper just under the sewn edge of the tape measure.

S is a vintage metal letter with black mini brads in the nail holes. **T** was made using a paper stencil. Buttons are the key ingredient in the letter **U**. **D** is actually an old game letter tile. To make the D larger, I added a stamped image of numbers layered on black cardstock and off-set the letter tile

for some added interest. I had a hard time with the **I** and tried several versions. I ended up cutting, one freehand wrapping it with copper wire, and layering it on some purple cardstock to add a color "pop." The **O** is a percolator part I found on a recent junking trip. The black seam binding adds a bit of definition to the letter. Once the measuring tape and letters were added, I was ready to start auditioning the other pieces.

fast! An optional and fun way to sew on pens, paintbrushes, or other pencil-like items to a quilt is to sew a piece of ribbon where you want to place the pen, then tie the ribbon around the item. You can either tie a knot or a bow, whichever best accents the item and the quilt. This tip works best for vertical embellishment.

Gallery of Quilts

More quilts from my friends and students
to inspire you.

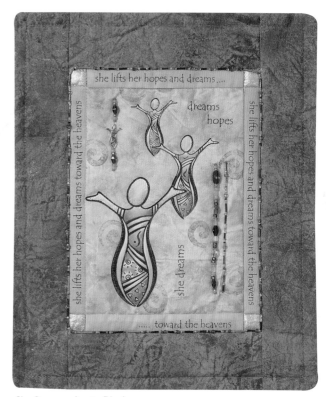

She Dreams, Angie Black

Autumn Memories, Darlene Domel and Sue Astroth

Untitled, Lari Drendell

Wisdom and Grace, Kathy Martin

The Rosen Girls Do London, Lucy Griljava

The UnQuilt, Zana Clark

Inspiration, Sue Astroth

Fun With Finishing Touches

There are several ways to hang your finished treasure. I started by hanging the quilts with a dowel and string.

First make a sleeve for the dowel. Cut a strip of fabric 5" wide and 1" shorter than the finished width of the quilt. Fold the fabric strip in half lengthwise, with wrong sides together. Sew a ¼" seam from the center of the strip out to each end. Leave a 2"-3" opening in the middle so you will be able to turn the piece right side out. Next, fold the strip in half with the seam in the center of the fabric.

Sew a ¼" seam to close each end of the strip and turn rightside out. Press. You are ready to sew the dowel pocket to the back of the quilt by hand. You do not have to sew the center opening closed because it will be sandwiched between the pocket and the back of the quilt.

I use a ¼" dowel a little longer than the finished measurement of the quilt. To hang my quilts I simply tie a thin cotton cord the length I need to each end of the dowel, adding a drop of glue to hold in place. Voila!

One of the easiest ways to hang a quilt is to find a great vintage hanger with clips.

Simply clip your quilt onto the hanger and you are set to go! This is a simple way to decorate when you want to change quilts for a new look, event, or holiday.

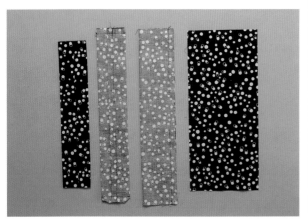

Making a sleeve

Another way to use old hangers is to sew the hanger directly to the quilt.

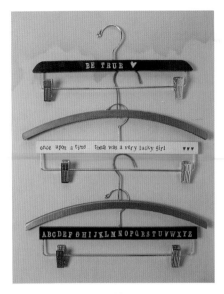

painted hanger

Painted hangers are a simple but effective way to display a quilt. Sand and wipe the hanger with a damp rag for a smooth and clean surface to paint. Paint with your favorite acrylic paint. Think about adding a personal touch with rubber stamps. I used stamps with pigment ink and heat set, using a heat tool available at craft stores. Be careful not to heat set too long or you will bubble your acrylic paint. Seal your hanger with an acrylic sealer to protect it.

Another way to hang your quilt is to frame it. Try lining the center of the frame with linen for an organic, natural look. You can also use an old bulletin board.

The Bingo Doll

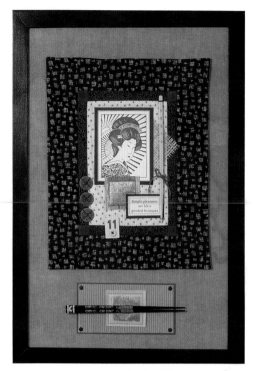

The Asian Quilted Frame

fun! Lining a picture frame is easy too. Just replace the center cardboard and glass with a piece of thin particleboard cut to size. The particleboard does make the frame a bit heavier so use brackets to hold the new fabric-covered center in place and eyelets and wire to hang on wall.

Labels

It doesn't matter how you add your name to your quilt, just make sure you do. You worked hard on it, so take the appropriate credit for it. Don't forget to add the date and name of your creation!

My favorite way to sign my quilts is to attach a tag that I have decorated to match the theme and sew it to the back. It's easy, quick, and a nice surprise for the person who turns the quilt over (and we all do that). Some other suggestions for signing your quilt include:

- ☐ Embroider the details directly onto the back of the quilt.
- ☐ Sign your name in beads.
- ☐ Iron a piece of muslin to some freezer paper and type out the information using a vintage typewriter.
- ☐ Sculpt your name in craft wire.
- ☐ Use game pieces to spell out your name.
- ☐ Use a handprint or fingerprint on paper and sign your name around the image, then layer and attach to quilt.
- ☐ Print out a paper label on the computer, layer onto cardstock, set eyelets in each corner, and attach to the back of the quilt.
- ☐ Rubber-stamp, your name and date on fabric, then appliqué to quilt.
- ☐ Using steel letters, stamp your name and date on a metal tag and sew it onto the quilt.

Storing Treasures in an Envelope

While working on the *Hawaii* quilt (page 44) I wanted to preserve the memories of a very special trip my family and I took to the Islands. We saw and did a lot and collected great souvenirs. There were too many souvenirs, in fact, to include on the front of the quilt. So I decided once I had the design I liked, I would decorate an envelope to hold pictures and a small journal of what we saw and shared on our trip.

I used a ready-made hanging tag envelope for the memory pocket. You can also make your own envelope using cardstock. There are many envelope templates on the market and wonderful papers to choose from to enhance your finished project. Here is a simple way to make a pocket, like the one on the school memories quilt.

1. Fold an 8½" x 11" sheet of paper lengthwise so the center panel is 4" and the side panels are 2⅛" and 2⅜", respectively.

2. Trim to the length pocket you want and then sew around 3 sides of the pocket.

3. Place 2 eyelets at the top 2 corners of the pocket so you can attach the pocket to the quilt back easily.

I created a pocket to fit a ready-made tag I purchased. You can adjust the size of your pocket to fit a tag, journal, or photo you may have.

I hope you are inspired by the numerous ideas, photos, and suggestions provided for finding treasures and making scrapbook quilts. Have fun, explore your own stash, go treasure hunting, spend some time at the machine, and see what you can come up with. Remember, anything is possible!

easy! Because I live with a nurse, and have great respect for the health of my body, I offer the following advice: Be sure to take breaks to stretch while you are working. I like to finish any project I start and will keep working even when my back is telling me to stop. Take a walk around the block, go get the mail, or just take a walk around the garden: You might just find inspiration for another quilt!

Resources

Thanks to all the artists and vendors that provided product and/or inspiration throughout this project:

Artists

Paula Best
www.paulabest.com

Suze Weinberg
www.schmoozewithsuze.com/

Zana Clark
www.stampzia.com

Kathy Martin
Postmoderndesigns@aol.com

Angie Black
www.angie-b-co.com

Janine Anderson
www.janineanderson.com

Stamp Companies

Artchix Studio
www.artchixstudio.com
1957 Hampshire Rd.
Victoria BC VSR 5T9
Canada

Beeswax
www.beeswaxrubberstamps.com

Club Scrap, Inc.
W6484 Design Dr.
Greenville, WI 54942
www.clubscrap.com

Hero Arts
1343 Powell St.
Emeryville, CA 94608
www.heroarts.com

Hampton Art Stamps
19 Industrial Blvd.
Medford, NY 11763
www.hamptonart.com

Judi-Kins, Inc.
17803 S. Harvard Blvd.
Gardena, CA 90248
www.judikins.com

Junque
P.O. Box 2378
Providence, RI 02906
www.junque.net

Just for Fun Rubber Stamps
301 E. Lemon Street
Tarpon Springs, FL 34689
www.jffstamps.com

Love to Stamp
3131 Dellrose Rd. SW
Tumwater, WA 98512

Lost Coast Designs
1079 O'Brien Court
San Jose, CA 95126-1046
www.lost-coast-designs.com

Ma Vinci's Reliquary
P.O. Box 472702
Aurora, CO 80047-2702
http://crafts.dm.net/mall/reliquary/

Oxford Impressions
P.O. Box 623
Oxford, MS 38655
www.oxfordimpressions.com

Paper Candy
P.O. Box 370422
Las Vegas, NV 80437
www.papercandy.com

Posh Impressions
22600-A Lambert St. #706
Lake Forest, CA 92630
www.poshimpressions.com

Postmodern Designs
P.O. Box 720416
Norman, OK 73070
e-mail postmoderndesign@aol.com

River City Rubber Works
5555 South Meridian
Wichita, KS 67217
www.rivercityrubberworks.com

Rubber Cottage
254 South Court St.
Medina, OH 44256
www.rubbercottage.com

Rubbernecker
932 Laroda Ct.
Ontario, CA 91762

A Stamp in the Hand
20507 S. Belshaw Avenue
Carson, CA 90746
www.astampinthehand.com

Stampers Anonymous
25967 Detroit Rd.
Westlake, OH 44145
www.stampersanonymous.com

Stampland
5033 N. Mozart St.
Chicago, IL 60625
www.stamplandchicago.com

Zettiology
P.O. Box 3329
Renton, WA 98056
www.zettiology.com

Other Sources

Paper Bliss Westrim: Great selection of ready-made embellishments and supplies for your scrapbook quilt projects www.westrimcrafts.com

Jolee EK Success: Wonderful ready-made embellishments for your scrapbook quilt projects www.eksuccess.com

Fiskars: Great line of fabric and paper scissors/cutters www.fiskars.com

Glue-Dots: A good way to attach embellishments to your quilts www.gluedots.com

Magenta Mesh: on no-sew quilt and a wonderful selection of rubber stamps www.magentarubberstamps.com

Making Memories: Great accessories and embellishments for your quilts www.makingmemories.com

Marvey Ink Pads and Punches: HYPERLINK "http://www.uchida.com" www.uchida.com

Colorbox: re-inkpads, reinkers, stamping accessories and stamp sheets www.clearsnap.com

White Sewing Machines: Mini sewing machines www.whitesewingmachines.com

JHB Buttons: Novelty, pearl, and metal buttons www.buttons.com

Tsukuniko: Ink pads and re-inkers www.tsukuniko.com

Great Online Fabric Shops

www.bighornquilts.com
www.hancocks-paducah.com
www.thebestkeptsecret.com
www.keepsakequilting.com
www.equilter.com
www.borntoquilt.com

Great shops to find Crafting Treasures

www.stamperswarehouse.com
www.joanns.com
www.michaels.com

Bibliography

McKelvey, Susan, and Janet Wickell, *Quilting and Color Made Easy.* Emmaus, PA: Rodale Inc., 2002.

Marion, Dan, *Designing with Notions.* Encino, CA: Autumn Leaves, 2002.

Miller, Joni K., and Lowry Thompson, *The Rubber Stamp Album.* New York: Workman Publishing Company, 1978.

Pearce, Amanda, *The Crafter's Complete Guide to Collage.* London Quarto Inc., 1997.

Trimble, Erin, *Designing With Textures.* Encino, CA: Autumn Leaves, 2002.

Wolfrom, Joen, *Color Play: Easy Steps to Imaginative Color in Quilts.* Lafayette, CA: C&T Publishing, 2002.

About the Author

Sue Astroth was born in southern California where she lived until seven years ago when she moved to, Concord, CA. She is the older of two kids; her brother Karl runs the family hardware and electronics store in the San Bernardino Mountains.

Sue has been a crafter all her life. She started out coloring, inside the lines of course. From crayons she moved to the needle arts. Her mom is a very talented needle artist as was her mom's mom, so it was a natural that Sue took up the craft. Sue started with felt dresses for her troll dolls trimmed

Photo by gregory case

with the best buttons the 60s had to offer. From there she tried knitting, embroidery, cross-stitch, and finally moved to sewing her own clothes. Her parents bought her first sewing machine in 1974 and in the early 80s she tried quilting. Mom and Dad included a craft and quilt store inside the existing hardware store. This endeavor encouraged Sue to make sample quilts for the store. She sold patterns for the store, as well as a couple of quilts too! Sue has been collecting fabric and making quilts ever since.

When Sue moved to the Bay Area, her quilts took a more artistic and eclectic turn. She also discovered the joy of treasure hunting at Bay Area flea markets and garage sales. She has managed to combine her love of quilting and treasure collecting in scrapbook quilts. When Sue isn't quilting, she is either in the garden or is working at a local stamp, art, and scrapbook store where she gets lots of great ideas.

Sue doesn't look back...except to say thank you for the good fortune she has had! She feels lucky to be surrounded by her family, many friends, and cute cat that love and encourage her to follow her dreams.

Index